MIND OV
COMPARISON

Overcoming Self-doubt and Comparisonitis

By

Dr Chris Ellis

ABOUT THE AUTHOR

Dr Chris Ellis is a therapist who has resolved issues in people's lives. He has solved issues between families, relationship issues, mental issues and the like. He's a therapist who helps people understand their emotions and regulate them.

TABLE OF CONTENTS

Recap of The Impact of Comparisonitis
Encouragement to Prioritize Self-Compassion and
a Growth Mindset

INTRODUCTION

In today's hyper-connected world, it's increasingly easy to fall into the trap of comparison. We find ourselves constantly bombarded with carefully curated images and updates from others, whether it's on social media, at work, or in our personal lives. As a result, we often find ourselves plagued by self-doubt and a pervasive sense of inadequacy. This phenomenon, known as "comparisonitis," has a profound impact on our mental health and well-being.

Comparisonitis can be defined as the relentless habit of measuring our worth and success against others, constantly finding ourselves falling short. It breeds self-doubt, perpetuates a negative self-image, and hampers our ability to recognize and appreciate our unique qualities and accomplishments. While it's natural to occasionally compare ourselves to others, comparisonitis takes it to an unhealthy extreme, leading to feelings of dissatisfaction, anxiety, and even depression.

Overcoming comparisonitis requires a shift in mindset—a conscious decision to prioritize our journey and embrace self-acceptance. It's about recognizing that our worth is not determined by how we measure up to others but by our intrinsic value and personal growth. This process requires us to harness the power of our minds to overcome self-doubt and cultivate a healthier perspective.

In this exploration of "Mind Over Comparison: Overcoming Self-Doubt and Comparisonitis," we will delve into the nature of comparisonitis, its negative consequences on our well-being, and the transformative power of the mind in combating it. We will uncover practical strategies and steps that can be taken to break free from the comparison trap, foster self-compassion, and embrace a growth mindset.

By embarking on this journey of self-discovery and empowerment, we can learn to appreciate our unique qualities, find fulfilment in our progress, and ultimately improve our mental health and overall well-being. Let us now embark on this transformative path, where the power of the mind triumphs over comparisonitis.

What Is Comparisonitis

Comparisonitis refers to the tendency to constantly compare oneself to others, often resulting in feelings of inferiority and low self-esteem. This phenomenon has become increasingly prevalent in today's society, with the rise of social media and the constant barrage of curated, filtered images and lifestyles.

Comparisonitis can manifest in various ways, such as constantly comparing one's appearance, achievements, relationships, or possessions to those of others. It can also lead to feelings of envy and jealousy, as well as a sense of inadequacy and self-doubt.

The negative effects of comparisonitis on mental health are significant, with studies linking it to increased levels of anxiety, depression, and overall psychological distress. It can also hinder personal growth and development by creating a fixed mindset focused on external validation and perfectionism.

Overcoming comparisonitis requires a shift in mindset and a focus on self-compassion and personal growth. It involves identifying triggers and limiting exposure to social media, cultivating a growth mindset, and practising self-care and self-compassion. Seeking support from friends, family, or a therapist can also help overcomeimproveonitis and improve mental health.

The Impact of Comparisonitis on Mental Health

Comparisonitis can have a significant impact on mental health. Constantly comparing oneself to others can lead to feelings of inferiority, low self-esteem, and self-doubt. When individuals perceive themselves as falling short in comparison to others, they may experience negative emotions such as envy, jealousy, and shame.

These negative emotions can lead to psychological distress and may contribute to the development of anxiety and depression. Studies have found that individuals who engage in social comparison are more likely to experience symptoms of anxiety and depression, particularly when the comparison is unfavourable.

Moreover, comparisonitis can create a fixed mindset that is focused on external validation and perfectionism, which can hinder personal growth and development. Individuals may become more concerned with achieving perfection and seeking approval from others, rather than focusing on their progress and goals.

Additionally, social media can exacerbate comparisonitis, as individuals are bombarded with curated, filtered images and lifestyles that can create unrealistic expectations and fuel comparison. The constant need to present oneself in a certain way on social media can also contribute to feelings of pressure and anxiety.

Overall, comparisonitis can have a detrimental impact on mental health, leading to negative emotions, psychological distress, and hindering personal growth and development. It is important to address comparisonitis and develop strategies to overcome it to promote positive mental health and well-being.

The Role of the Mind in Overcoming Comparisonitis

The mind plays a crucial role in overcoming comparisonitis, as it influences how individuals perceive themselves and their surroundings. The way individuals think and perceive their experiences can have a significant impact on their mental health, particularly when it comes to social comparison.

Developing a growth mindset is one-way individuals can use the power of their minds to overcome comparisonitis. A growth mindset emphasizes the potential for growth and improvement, rather than a fixed mindset that focuses on innate abilities and external validation. With a growth mindset, individuals can focus on their progress and development, rather than comparing themselves to others.

Another important aspect of the mind in overcoming comparisonitis is self-compassion. Self-compassion involves treating oneself with kindness, understanding, and acceptance, rather than harsh self-judgment and criticism. By practising self-compassion, individuals can develop a more positive self-image and reduce the negative impact of social comparison.

Mindfulness is also a powerful tool in overcoming comparisonitis. Mindfulness involves being present at the moment and non-judgmentally observing one's thoughts and feelings. By practicing mindfulness, individuals can become more aware of their thoughts and emotions, and learn to observe them without becoming overwhelmed or attached to them.

In addition, reframing one's thoughts can also be an effective way to overcome comparisonitis. Instead of focusing on what others have or what one lacks, individuals can reframe their thoughts to focus on what they have achieved, or what they can do to improve themselves. This positive reframing can help to reduce negative emotions and shift the focus to personal growth and development.

In conclusion, the mind plays a crucial role in overcoming comparisonitis. By developing a growth mindset, practising self-compassion, and mindfulness, and reframing one's thoughts, individuals can reduce the negative impact of social comparison, promote positive mental health, and focus on their personal growth and development.

CHAPTER ONE

The Nature of Comparisonitis

The nature of comparisonitis encompasses the underlying factors and dynamics associated with the tendency to engage in constant comparison with others. It involves the cognitive and emotional processes that drive individuals to evaluate themselves about others and often leads to feelings of inferiority, low self-esteem, and self-doubt.

One aspect of the nature of comparisonitis is the innate human tendency to compare oneself to others. From an evolutionary perspective, humans have a natural inclination to assess their social standing and compare themselves to others as a way to gauge their success, abilities, and worth. This tendency served as a survival mechanism in the past, allowing individuals to assess their relative strengths and weaknesses within their social group.

In contemporary society, comparisonitis is further fueled by various societal factors. Social media platforms, in particular, have become a breeding ground for comparison. People often present carefully curated versions of their lives, showcasing only the highlights and achievements. This creates an environment where individuals are constantly exposed to idealized representations of others' lives, leading to an increased likelihood of unfavourable social comparisons.

The psychological effects of comparisonitis are profound. Individuals who engage in frequent social comparisons may experience negative emotions such as envy, jealousy, and dissatisfaction. They may perceive themselves as falling short in comparison to others, leading to feelings of inadequacy and a diminished sense of self-worth. This negative emotional impact can have detrimental effects on mental health, contributing to increased levels of anxiety, depression, and overall psychological distress.

Comparisonitis can also hinder personal growth and development. By constantly focusing on others' achievements and appearances, individuals may become preoccupied with seeking external validation and trying to measure up to unrealistic standards. This fixed mindset can inhibit one's progress and undermine the pursuit of personal goals, as the focus becomes centred on outperforming others rather than self-improvement and intrinsic fulfilment.

Furthermore, comparisonitis can perpetuate a cycle of self-doubt and dissatisfaction. The more individuals engage in social comparison, the more they reinforce negative thought patterns and beliefs about themselves. This can create a self-perpetuating cycle of seeking validation, experiencing disappointment, and further comparison, leading to a continuous cycle of negative self-perception.

In conclusion, the nature of comparisonitis involves a combination of innate human tendencies, societal influences, and the psychological effects it has on individuals. Understanding and addressing the underlying factors driving comparisonitis are essential to overcome its negative impact on self-esteem, mental health, and personal growth.

Why do we Compare Ourselves to Others

The act of comparing ourselves with others is deeply ingrained in human nature and stems from a variety of psychological and social factors. Understanding why we engage in this behaviour can shed light on the motivations behind it. Here are some reasons why we compare ourselves with others:

1. Social Comparison Theory: Developed by social psychologist Leon Festinger, the Social Comparison Theory suggests that humans have an inherent drive to evaluate their own opinions, abilities, and attributes by comparing themselves to others. We often seek information from others to gauge our performance and determine our self-worth. By comparing ourselves with others, we gain insights into how we measure up and where we stand with our peers.

2. Self-Evaluation and Identity Formation: Comparisons provide a reference point for self-evaluation. We tend to define ourselves through social interactions and by comparing ourselves with others. This process helps us shape our identity, develop a sense of belonging, and understand our strengths and weaknesses. Comparisons can offer insights into our abilities, accomplishments, and potential for growth.

3. Normative Social Influence: Humans are influenced by social norms and societal expectations. Comparing ourselves with others helps us determine what is considered "normal" or "desirable" within a given context. By conforming to these norms, we seek acceptance and validation from our social groups. This drive to fit in and meet societal expectations often leads to comparing ourselves with others who embody the qualities or achievements we desire.

4. Personal Validation and Self-Esteem: Comparison can serve as a source of personal validation. When we perceive ourselves as superior or more successful than others, it can boost our self-esteem and provide a sense of accomplishment. On the other hand, unfavourable comparisons may lead to feelings of inferiority and diminished self-worth. By seeking validation through comparison, we attempt to validate our existence and worthiness.

5. Aspiration and Motivation: Comparisons can serve as a source of inspiration and motivation. When we observe others who have achieved what we aspire to accomplish, it can ignite a desire for self-improvement and drive us to set higher goals. Comparisons can provide a benchmark for progress and push us to strive for excellence.

6. Social Influence and Competition: The competitive nature of human society often fuels the desire to compare ourselves with others. In a society that values achievements, wealth, and status, we engage in comparisons to assess our relative position and compete for limited resources. Comparisons can fuel ambition, encourage personal growth, and drive us to excel in various domains.

While comparison can be a natural and sometimes beneficial process, it is important to recognize when it becomes detrimental to our well-being. Excessive or unhealthy comparisons can lead to feelings of inadequacy, jealousy, and self-doubt. Developing a healthy perspective on comparison involves cultivating self-awareness, focusing on personal growth, and practising self-compassion. By understanding the motivations behind our comparisons, we can navigate them in a way that promotes positive self-perception and supports our overall well-being.

The Psychological Effects of Comparisonitis

Comparisonitis, the constant habit of comparing oneself to others, can have significant psychological effects on individuals. These effects can be detrimental to mental health and well-being. Here are some of the psychological effects of comparisonitis:

1. Decreased Self-Esteem: Comparisonitis often leads to a diminished sense of self-esteem. When individuals continuously compare themselves to others and perceive themselves as falling short, it reinforces feelings of inadequacy and lowers their self-worth. Constantly measuring oneself against others can create a negative self-image and erode self-confidence.

2. Increased Stress and Anxiety: Comparisonitis is often accompanied by heightened levels of stress and anxiety. Individuals may feel constant pressure to measure up to the perceived achievements or qualities of others. This pressure can lead to chronic stress and anxiety as they strive to meet unrealistic standards, fearing that they will never be good enough.

3. Negative Emotions: Engaging in comparisonitis can evoke a range of negative emotions. Envy, jealousy, and resentment are common emotional responses when individuals perceive others as having more success, happiness, or possessions. These negative emotions can cause significant distress and detract from one's ability to experience contentment and gratitude.

4. Perfectionism: Comparisonitis can fuel perfectionistic tendencies. When individuals constantly compare themselves to others, they may develop a mindset that demands flawless performance and achievement. The fear of falling short and being judged unfavourably can lead to perfectionism, which can be debilitating and hinder personal growth and satisfaction.

5. Impaired Self-Identity: Comparisonitis can blur one's sense of self-identity. When individuals primarily define themselves based on external comparisons, they may struggle to develop a strong, authentic self-concept. This can lead to feelings of confusion, lack of direction, and a diminished understanding of their values, strengths, and goals.

6. Impacted Relationships: Constant comparison with others can strain relationships. Individuals may feel envious or resentful towards those they perceive as more successful or fortunate. These feelings can negatively impact interpersonal dynamics, causing distance, animosity, or strained social connections.

7. Reduced Life Satisfaction: Comparisonitis can diminish overall life satisfaction. By consistently focusing on what others have or what one lacks, individuals may struggle to appreciate their accomplishments and experiences. This constant comparison can prevent them from finding contentment and happiness in their own lives.

It is important to recognize and address the psychological effects of comparisonitis. Developing self-awareness, cultivating self-compassion, and practising gratitude can help individuals counteract the negative impacts of comparison. Embracing one's unique journey, setting realistic goals, and focusing on personal growth can lead to a more positive mindset and improved mental well-being.

The Role of Social Media in Exacerbating Comparisonitis

Social media plays a significant role in exacerbating comparisonitis, intensifying the tendency to compare oneself with others. The pervasive presence and influence of social media platforms have created a breeding ground for comparison and self-doubt. Here are some key ways in which social media contributes to the exacerbation of comparisonitis:

1. Highlight Reels and Idealized Representations: Social media platforms often present curated and idealized versions of people's lives. Users tend to showcase their best moments, achievements, and desirable aspects of their lives, creating a distorted reality. The constant exposure to these highlight reels can lead individuals to compare their own lives, achievements, and appearances to these seemingly perfect depictions, fueling feelings of inadequacy and self-doubt.

2. Filtered and Edited Images: The widespread use of filters, editing tools, and photo manipulation on social media platforms contributes to an unrealistic portrayal of beauty and physical appearance. People often enhance their images to present an idealized version of themselves. When individuals see these altered images, they may compare their own unfiltered and unedited appearances, leading to negative body image and self-esteem issues.

3. Selective Sharing and FOMO: Social media platforms often create a fear of missing out (FOMO) among users. People tend to share exciting and positive experiences, such as travel, parties, or achievements, which can generate a sense of exclusion or inadequacy in those who view them. Seeing others enjoying exciting activities or seemingly having a better social life can intensify the desire to compare and question one's own life choices or experiences.

4. Quantifiable Metrics of Success: Social media platforms often emphasize quantifiable metrics of success, such as followers, likes, comments, and shares. These metrics can become a measure of popularity and validation. Individuals may compare their numbers and engagement to others, leading to feelings of inferiority or a diminished sense of self-worth if they perceive themselves as "less successful" in terms of these metrics.

5. Unrealistic Standards and Influencer Culture: Influencers and celebrities on social media often set unrealistic standards for beauty, lifestyle, and success. Their carefully curated content can create an aspirational ideal that is difficult for most people to attain. Constant exposure to these unattainable standards can intensify comparisonitis, as individuals strive to achieve a similar level of success or appearance, even if it is unrealistic or unattainable.

6. Constant Availability and Comparison Loop: Social media platforms provide a constant stream of content and updates from others. The never-ending scrolling and exposure to other people's lives can lead to a continuous loop of comparison. This constant availability reinforces the habit of comparison and makes it challenging for individuals to escape the cycle of comparisonitis.

To mitigate the negative impact of social media on comparisonitis, individuals can employ various strategies. These include practising digital detoxes, limiting social media use, curating their feeds to include positive and diverse content, practising self-awareness and self-compassion, and focusing on authentic connections and offline experiences. By being mindful of the role social media plays in exacerbating comparisonitis, individuals can take steps to protect their mental well-being and cultivate a healthier relationship with social media.

CHAPTER TWO

The Negative Consequences of Comparisonitis

Comparisonitis, the constant habit of comparing oneself to others, can have a range of negative consequences that can significantly impact an individual's well-being and overall quality of life. Here are some of the negative consequences of comparisonitis:

1. Diminished Self-Esteem: Comparisonitis often leads to a decrease in self-esteem. When individuals constantly compare themselves to others and perceive themselves as falling short, it reinforces feelings of inadequacy and lowers their self-worth. The constant focus on others' achievements, appearances, or possessions can create a negative self-image, eroding self-confidence and contributing to a diminished sense of personal value.

2. Increased Stress and Anxiety: Engaging in comparisonitis is often accompanied by heightened levels of stress and anxiety. The pressure to measure up to perceived achievements or qualities of others can create a chronic sense of stress. Individuals may experience anxiety related to the fear of not meeting societal or personal expectations, leading to feelings of inadequacy and a constant sense of unease.

3. Negative Emotions: Comparisonitis evokes a range of negative emotions. Envy, jealousy, and resentment are common emotional responses when individuals perceive others as having more success, happiness, or possessions. These negative emotions can cause significant distress and detract from one's ability to experience contentment and genuine happiness.

4. Damaged Self-Image: Constantly comparing oneself to others can damage self-image and lead to a distorted perception of oneself. Individuals may develop an unrealistic and unfavourable view of their abilities, accomplishments, or physical appearance. This can create a negative cycle of self-criticism and self-doubt, hindering personal growth and impeding the pursuit of one's goals.

5. Impaired Mental Health: Comparisonitis can contribute to the development or exacerbation of mental health issues. The constant self-evaluation and negative comparisons can contribute to symptoms of anxiety, depression, and other mental health disorders. The persistent focus on others' achievements and perceived shortcomings can lead to a sense of hopelessness and a negative outlook on life.

6. Strained Relationships: Comparisonitis can strain relationships, both with others and with oneself. Constantly comparing oneself to others can create feelings of envy, competition, and resentment, which can negatively impact interpersonal dynamics. These negative feelings can lead to distance, animosity, or strained social connections.

7. Reduced Life Satisfaction: Comparisonitis detracts from one's ability to experience genuine satisfaction and contentment in life. By constantly comparing oneself to others and focusing on what one lacks or what others have, individuals may struggle to appreciate their accomplishments and experiences. This constant comparison can prevent them from finding true fulfilment and happiness in their own lives.

It is important to recognize and address the negative consequences of comparisonitis. Developing self-awareness, cult and activating self-compassion and practising gratitude can help individuals counteract the negative impacts of comparison. By shifting the focus to personal growth, self-acceptance, and genuine connections with others, individuals can foster a more positive and fulfilling life experience.

How Comparisonitis Affects Self-esteem

Comparisonitis, the constant habit of comparing oneself to others, can have a profound impact on self-esteem. Self-esteem refers to an individual's overall evaluation of their worth and value. Here is an in-depth exploration of how comparisonitis affects self-esteem:

1. Negative Social Comparisons: Comparisonitis often leads to negative social comparisons, where individuals perceive themselves as inferior or lacking in comparison to others. Constantly evaluating oneself based on external factors, such as achievements, possessions, or appearance, can create a sense of inadequacy and diminish self-esteem. When individuals consistently believe they fall short in comparison to others, it erodes their self-confidence and leads to a negative self-perception.

2. Unattainable Standards: Comparisonitis often involves comparing oneself to idealized versions of others. Social media, for instance, presents curated and edited representations of people's lives, which can create unrealistic standards for success, beauty, or happiness. Individuals may feel compelled to measure up to these unattainable standards, which can be damaging to self-esteem when they inevitably fall short.

3. Self-Worth Based on External Factors: Comparisonitis reinforces the notion that one's self-worth is contingent upon external factors, such as achievements or material possessions. When individuals constantly compare themselves to others and base their self-worth on these external markers, their self-esteem becomes dependent on external validation. This can be a fragile foundation for self-esteem, as it leaves individuals vulnerable to fluctuations in comparison to others.

4. Negative Self-Talk and Internal Criticism: Engaging in comparisonitis often leads to negative self-talk and internal criticism. Individuals may engage in self-deprecating thoughts, constantly belittling their achievements or qualities when comparing themselves to others. This internal dialogue reinforces negative self-perceptions and erodes self-esteem over time.

5. Perceived Inadequacy and Self-Doubt: Comparisonitis fosters a sense of inadequacy and self-doubt. When individuals consistently compare themselves to others and perceive themselves as falling short, it fuels feelings of not being good enough. These feelings of inadequacy can chip away at self-esteem, creating a cycle of self-doubt and diminishing one's belief in their capabilities and worth.

6. Disrupted Self-Identity: Comparisonitis can disrupt the development of a healthy self-identity. When individuals primarily define themselves through external comparisons, they may struggle to cultivate a strong sense of self and an authentic self-concept. Their self-esteem becomes contingent upon how they measure up to others, rather than being rooted in their unique qualities and values.

7. Limited Self-Acceptance: Comparisonitis inhibits self-acceptance and self-compassion. When individuals constantly compare themselves to others, they may focus on their perceived flaws or shortcomings, leading to self-criticism and a lack of self-acceptance. This self-judgment hampers self-esteem, as individuals struggle to appreciate and value themselves as they are.

To address the negative impact of comparisonitis on self-esteem, individuals can cultivate self-awareness, practice self-compassion, and focus on their progress and growth rather than comparing themselves to others. It is important to recognize that self-esteem should be based on internal validation, self-acceptance, and a realistic appraisal of one's strengths and accomplishments. By fostering a positive and supportive inner dialogue and nurturing a sense of intrinsic self-worth, individuals can protect and enhance their self-esteem in the face of comparisonitis.

The Link Between Comparisonitis and Anxiety and Depression

Comparisonitis, the constant habit of comparing oneself to others, is closely linked to anxiety and depression. The pervasive nature of comparison and its impact on self-worth and psychological well-being contribute to the development and exacerbation of these mental health conditions. Here is a comprehensive exploration of the link between comparisonitis and anxiety and depression:

1. Perceived Inadequacy and Self-Doubt: Comparisonitis fosters a sense of inadequacy and self-doubt as individuals constantly compare themselves to others and perceive themselves as falling short. This constant self-evaluation and negative comparisons can lead to a chronic state of self-doubt, where individuals question their worth and capabilities. This self-doubt is a significant contributing factor to both anxiety and depression.

2. Unattainable Standards and Unrealistic Expectations: Comparisonitis often involves comparing oneself to idealized versions of others, which can create unrealistic standards for success, beauty, or happiness. When individuals feel pressure to measure up to these unattainable standards, it can lead to chronic stress and anxiety. The fear of not meeting societal or personal expectations can contribute to the development of anxiety disorders and worsen existing anxiety symptoms. Similarly, the constant striving for unattainable goals can lead to a sense of hopelessness and contribute to depressive symptoms.

3. Negative Self-Image and Low Self-Esteem: Comparisonitis can significantly impact self-image and self-esteem. Constantly comparing oneself to others and perceiving oneself as inferior can erode self-esteem and create a negative self-image. Low self-esteem is closely associated with both anxiety and depression. It can lead to feelings of worthlessness, self-criticism, and a distorted view of oneself, all of which contribute to the development and maintenance of these mental health conditions.

4. Rumination and Overthinking: Engaging in comparisonitis often involves rumination and overthinking. Individuals may continuously analyze and ruminate over their own perceived shortcomings or failures in comparison to others. This rumination prolongs negative thought patterns and intensifies feelings of anxiety and depression. The constant focus on comparison can also lead to overthinking and excessive worrying about one's inadequacies, further exacerbating symptoms of anxiety and depression.

5. Social Isolation and Withdrawal: Comparisonitis can lead to social isolation and withdrawal from social activities. Individuals may feel a sense of shame, embarrassment, or a fear of judgment when they believe they don't measure up to others. This social withdrawal can contribute to feelings of loneliness, which are strongly linked to anxiety and depression. Lack of social support and connection further exacerbates these mental health conditions.

6. Cognitive Distortions: Comparisonitis often involves cognitive distortions, such as overgeneralization, black-and-white thinking, and magnifying one's flaws while minimizing strengths. These distortions contribute to negative thinking patterns that are characteristic of anxiety and depression. The constant comparison with others reinforces these cognitive distortions, leading to a perpetuation of negative thoughts and emotions.

7. Reduced Life Satisfaction: Comparisonitis detracts from an individual's ability to experience genuine satisfaction and contentment in life. Constantly comparing oneself to others and focusing on what one lacks can prevent individuals from appreciating their accomplishments and experiences. This can contribute to feelings of dissatisfaction and hopelessness, which are common features of depression.

It is crucial to recognize the link between comparisonitis and anxiety and depression to address and manage these mental health conditions effectively. Developing self-awareness, cultivating self-compassion, and challenging negative thought patterns are essential steps in overcoming the negative impact of comparisonitis. Seeking professional help, such as therapy or counselling, can also provide valuable support in managing anxiety and depression associated with comparisonitis.

How Comparisonitis Hinders Personal Growth and Development

Comparisonitis, the constant habit of comparing oneself to others, can significantly hinder personal growth and development. While striving for self-improvement and learning from others can be beneficial, comparisonitis tends to have a negative impact. Here's a comprehensive exploration of how comparisonitis hinders personal growth and development:

1. Distorted Self-Perception: Comparisonitis distorts an individual's self-perception. Constantly comparing oneself to others often leads to an unrealistic and unfavourable view of one's abilities, accomplishments, or appearance. This distorted self-perception can undermine self-confidence and discourage individuals from pursuing new opportunities or challenges, hindering personal growth.

2. Fear of Failure and Risk Aversion: Comparisonitis breeds a fear of failure and risk aversion. When individuals constantly compare themselves to others, they may become overly cautious and hesitant to take risks. The fear of not measuring up to others or the fear of failure can paralyze individuals, preventing them from stepping out of their comfort zones and inhibiting personal growth.

3. Self-Limiting Beliefs: Comparisonitis reinforces self-limiting beliefs. Individuals may develop beliefs such as "I'll never be as good as them" or "I'm not talented enough." These beliefs create mental barriers that impede personal growth and development. By internalizing these self-limiting beliefs, individuals may resist trying new things, pursuing their passions, or taking on challenges that could facilitate growth.

4. Lack of Authenticity: Comparisonitis can lead to a lack of authenticity. When individuals constantly compare themselves to others, they may feel pressured to conform to societal or perceived expectations. This can result in the suppression of one's true identity and the adoption of a persona that aligns with the perceived "ideal." Inauthenticity hinders personal growth as individuals are not fully embracing their unique qualities and pursuing paths that align with their true values and aspirations.

5. Focus on External Validation: Comparisonitis perpetuates a focus on external validation. When individuals constantly compare themselves to others, they seek external validation and approval to feel a sense of worth. This external validation becomes a driving force in decision-making and personal growth, rather than relying on internal motivations and personal fulfilment. By seeking validation from others, individuals may lose sight of their intrinsic desires and hinder their personal development.

6. Negative Mindset and Self-Criticism: Engaging in comparisonitis often leads to a negative mindset and self-criticism. Individuals may engage in constant self-comparison and self-judgment, focusing on their perceived shortcomings or failures. This negative mindset and self-criticism create a hostile environment for personal growth, as individuals may become overly self-critical and avoid taking risks or pursuing opportunities for fear of falling short.

7. Missed Opportunities for Learning and Collaboration: Comparisonitis can lead to missed opportunities for learning and collaboration. When individuals are consumed by comparison, they may overlook the value of learning from others or collaborating with them. By solely focusing on outperforming or measuring up to others, individuals miss the chance to benefit from diverse perspectives, insights, and skills that can facilitate personal growth and development.

To overcome the hindrances caused by comparisonitis, individuals can practice self-awareness, cultivate self-compassion, and shift their focus to internal growth and progress. Embracing one's unique journey, setting personal goals, and celebrating individual achievements can foster personal growth. It's important to remember that each individual has their timeline and path, and personal development should be driven by intrinsic motivations rather than comparisons to others.

CHAPTER THREE

The Power of The Mind in Overcoming Comparisonitis

The power of the mind plays a crucial role in overcoming comparisonitis, the constant habit of comparing oneself to others. By harnessing the strength of the mind, individuals can break free from the negative cycle of comparison and cultivate a healthier, more fulfilling mindset. Here's an exploration of the power of the mind in overcoming comparisonitis:

1. Self-Awareness: The first step in overcoming comparisonitis is developing self-awareness. The mind can observe and recognize when comparisonitis arises within oneself. By being aware of the tendency to compare and its detrimental effects, individuals can take conscious steps to redirect their thoughts and focus on their growth and progress.

2. Thought Awareness and Reframing: The mind has the power to observe and control thoughts. By becoming aware of the thoughts associated with comparisonitis, individuals can challenge and reframe them. Instead of dwelling on negative comparisons, individuals can choose to replace those thoughts with positive affirmations and self-encouragement. This shift in mindset allows for a more constructive and empowering perspective.

3. Cultivating Self-Compassion: The mind can be trained to cultivate self-compassion, which is a powerful tool in overcoming comparisonitis. Rather than engaging in self-criticism or self-judgment, individuals can use the power of the mind to show kindness and understanding to themselves. Embracing self-compassion allows individuals to acknowledge their worth and appreciate their unique journey, reducing the need for comparison with others.

4. Focus on Personal Growth: The mind can shift focus from external comparisons to personal growth. By redirecting attention to one's progress and development, individuals can channel their energy towards setting and achieving personal goals. The mind can be trained to prioritize self-improvement rather than constantly comparing oneself to others, leading to a sense of fulfilment and accomplishment.

5. Gratitude Practice: The mind can cultivate gratitude as a powerful antidote to comparisonitis. By training the mind to focus on what one has rather than what one lacks, individuals can develop a mindset of gratitude. Practising gratitude helps individuals appreciate their own blessings, strengths, and unique qualities, reducing the need for comparison and fostering contentment.

6. Mindfulness and Present Moment Awareness: The mind has the capacity for mindfulness, which involves being fully present at the moment without judgment. By practising mindfulness, individuals can cultivate awareness of their thoughts and emotions, allowing them to detach from comparisonitis and the associated negative emotions. Mindfulness empowers individuals to redirect their attention to the present moment, embracing their own experiences and letting go of the need to compare.

7. Positive Self-Talk and Affirmations: The mind can be harnessed to engage in positive self-talk and affirmations. By consciously choosing uplifting and empowering words, individuals can rewire their thought patterns and replace self-limiting beliefs with positive and encouraging statements. Positive self-talk boosts self-esteem, fosters self-belief, and helps individuals overcome the harmful effects of comparisonitis.

By harnessing the power of the mind, individuals can break free from the grip of comparisonitis. Through self-awareness, reframing thoughts, cultivating self-compassion, focusing on personal growth, practising gratitude, and mindfulness, and engaging in positive self-talk, individuals can develop a healthier mindset that supports their well-being and allows them to appreciate their unique journey. The mind becomes a powerful ally in overcoming comparisonitis and embracing personal fulfilment.

The Role of The Mindset in Overcoming Comparisonitis

The role of mindset is paramount in overcoming comparisonitis, the constant habit of comparing oneself to others. By cultivating a resilient and empowering mindset, individuals can effectively break free from the negative cycle of comparison and develop a healthier perspective. Here's an exploration of the role of mindset in overcoming comparisonitis:

1. Awareness Mindset: Developing an awareness mindset is crucial in overcoming comparisonitis. It involves being consciously aware of one's thouemotionsotions, and behaviours related to comparison. By adopting an awareness mindset, individuals can catch themselves in the act of comparing and bringing their attention back to the present moment. This mindfulness allows for a shift in focus from external comparisons to internal growth.

2. Growth Mindset: Cultivating a growth mindset is instrumental in overcoming comparisonitis. A growth mindset is characterized by the belief that abilities and intelligence can be developed through dedication and effort. Individuals with a growth mindset see failures and setbacks as opportunities for learning and growth. By embracing a growth mindset, individuals can shift their focus from comparing themselves to others to focusing on their progress and continuous improvement.

3. Gratitude Mindset: A gratitude mindset plays a significant role in overcoming comparisonitis. By cultivating an attitude of gratitude, individuals shift their focus from what they lack to what they appreciate and value in their own lives. A gratitude mindset helps individuals develop contentment, reducing the need for constant comparison and fostering a sense of fulfilment based on personal blessings and achievements.

4. Self-Compassion Mindset: Developing a self-compassion mindset is vital in overcoming comparisonitis. It involves treating oneself with kindness, understanding, and acceptance. Individuals with a self-compassion mindset acknowledge their worthiness and embrace their unique qualities and journey. By practising self-compassion, individuals can counteract self-criticism and reduce the need to compare themselves to others.

5. Abundance Mindset: Adopting an abundance mindset is instrumental in overcoming comparisonitis. An abundance mindset is rooted in the belief that there is enough success, happiness, and fulfilment for everyone. It counters the scarcity mindset that fuels comparison and competition. By embracing an abundance mindset, individuals celebrate the successes and achievements of others without feeling threatened or inadequate, fostering a supportive and positive outlook.

6. Authenticity Mindset: Cultivating an authenticity mindset is crucial in overcoming comparisonitis. It involves embracing one's true self and values, rather than conforming to external expectations. Individuals with an authenticity mindset prioritize self-expression and genuine connections over the need for approval or comparison. By focusing on living authentically, individuals can overcome the pressures of comparison and cultivate a sense of fulfilment based on their own unique identity.

7. Positive Mindset and Affirmations:
Maintaining a positive mindset and engaging in positive affirmations play a vital role in overcoming comparisonitis. By consciously choosing uplifting and empowering thoughts and affirmations, individuals can rewire their thought patterns and counteract self-limiting beliefs. Positive mindset and affirmations foster self-belief, boost self-esteem, and create a positive internal dialogue that supports personal growth and well-being.

By embracing these mindsets, individuals can overcome comparisonitis and develop a healthier perspective. Mindsets centred around awareness, growth, gratitude, self-compassion, abundance, authenticity, and positivity empower individuals to focus on their journey, appreciate their unique qualities, and cultivate personal fulfilment. The role of mindset in overcoming comparisonitis is transformative, allowing individuals to break free from the harmful effects of comparison and embrace a more fulfilling and authentic life.

Strategies for Cultivating a Growth Mindset

Cultivating a growth mindset is a powerful strategy for personal development and overcoming challenges. It involves adopting a belief that intelligence, abilities, and skills can be developed through dedication, effort, and learning. Here are several strategies to help cultivate a growth mindset:

1. Embrace Challenges: See challenges as opportunities for growth rather than obstacles. Embrace them as chances to learn, develop new skills, and expand your knowledge. Embracing challenges with a positive attitude allows you to approach them as stepping stones to personal growth.

2. Adopt a Positive Attitude Towards Failure: Instead of viewing failure as a reflection of your abilities, see it as a valuable learning experience. Embrace failures as opportunities to gain insights, adjust your approach, and improve for future endeavours. Emphasize the process of learning and growing rather than solely focusing on the outcome.

3. Practice Persistence and Effort: Understand that achieving mastery or success requires effort and dedication. Cultivate a mindset that values perseverance and putting in the necessary work. Recognize that progress may be gradual and that setbacks are part of the learning process. Maintain a commitment to continuous improvement and keep striving toward your goals.

4. Foster a Love for Learning: Develop a curiosity and passion for learning. See every experience as an opportunity to gain new knowledge and skills. Embrace a lifelong learning mindset, seeking out new information, seeking feedback, and being open to new perspectives. Continuously expand your knowledge base and challenge yourself to acquire new skills.

5. Emphasize the Power of Yet: Replace "I can't" with "I can't yet." Embrace the belief that your abilities can be developed with time and effort. Recognize that setbacks or limitations are temporary, and with perseverance, you can achieve your goals. The word "yet" instils a sense of possibility and encourages a growth-oriented mindset.

6. Surround Yourself with Growth-Oriented Individuals: Surrounding yourself with people who have a growth mindset can significantly impact your mindset. Seek out individuals who inspire you, challenge you, and believe in the power of growth and development. Engage in discussions and collaborations that encourage learning, resilience, and personal growth.

7. Cultivate Self-Reflection and Self-Awareness: Take time for self-reflection and self-awareness. Notice your thoughts, beliefs, and self-talk. Challenge any fixed mindset tendencies or negative self-perceptions. Cultivate a mindset of self-compassion, where you acknowledge your efforts, progress, and strengths. Use self-reflection as an opportunity to identify areas for growth and set actionable goals.

8. Practice Mindfulness: Engage in mindfulness practices to cultivate awareness of your thoughts and emotions. Mindfulness allows you to observe any fixed mindset tendencies and consciously choose to shift to a growth mindset. By staying present and non-judgmental, you can develop a greater sense of self-awareness and respond to challenges with a growth-oriented perspective.

9. Celebrate Effort and Progress: Focus on celebrating your efforts, progress, and small wins along the way. Acknowledge the hard work and dedication you put into your growth and development. Celebrating progress reinforces the idea that growth is achievable and encourages you to continue striving for improvement.

10. Learn from Mentors and Role Models: Seek guidance and inspiration from mentors or role models who embody a growth mindset. Study their journeys, their approaches to challenges, and how they view setbacks. Learning from those who have achieved success through a growth-oriented mindset can provide valuable insights and motivation.

By implementing these strategies consistently, you can cultivate a growth mindset and unlock your potential for personal and professional growth. Remember that developing a growth mindset is an ongoing process, and with practice, you can transform the way you approach challenges and embrace a mindset of continuous learning and development.

The Importance of Self-compassion in Combating Comparisonitis

Self-compassion plays a crucial role in combating comparisonitis, the harmful habit of constantly comparing oneself to others. Comparisonitis often leads to negative self-judgment, feelings of inadequacy, and a decrease in self-worth. In such situations, self-compassion acts as a powerful antidote, promoting emotional well-being and resilience. Here's an exploration of the importance of self-compassion in combating comparisonitis:

1. Reduces Self-Criticism: Comparisonitis often triggers self-critical thoughts and beliefs about one's abilities or accomplishments. Self-compassion helps counteract this by offering kindness and understanding towards oneself. Instead of engaging in self-blame or harsh self-criticism, self-compassion allows individuals to approach their perceived shortcomings or failures with a gentle and non-judgmental attitude.

2. Fosters Self-Acceptance: Comparisonitis often stems from a desire to conform to external standards or ideals. Self-compassion encourages self-acceptance by recognizing and embracing one's unique qualities, strengths, and limitations. It cultivates an understanding that everyone has their journey, and it is okay to be imperfect. Self-acceptance promotes a sense of self-worth and reduces the need for constant comparison with others.

3. Provides Emotional Support: Comparisonitis can trigger feelings of insecurity, envy, and frustration. Self-compassion offers emotional support during these challenging moments. It involves extending kindness, care, and empathy towards oneself, and acknowledging that these feelings are valid and understandable. Self-compassion provides a nurturing and safe space for individuals to process their emotions and find comfort in difficult times.

4. Encourages Mindfulness and Present Moment Awareness: Self-compassion is closely linked to mindfulness and present-moment awareness. By practising self-compassion, individuals become more attuned to their thoughts and emotions related to comparisonitis. They can observe these thoughts without judgment, bringing their attention back to the present moment. This mindful awareness allows individuals to disengage from comparison and cultivate a more compassionate and balanced perspective.

5. Promotes Healthy Self-Esteem: Comparisonitis can erode self-esteem, as individuals constantly measure themselves against others and often come up short. Self-compassion fosters healthy self-esteem by acknowledging one's inherent worth and valuing oneself regardless of external comparisons. It shifts the focus from external validation to self-acceptance and self-love, promoting a positive sense of self.

6. Cultivates Resilience: Comparisonitis can be emotionally draining and hinder personal growth. Self-compassion builds resilience by providing individuals with the emotional resources to bounce back from setbacks and challenges. It encourages individuals to treat themselves with kindness and understanding during difficult times, fostering a sense of inner strength and the ability to navigate comparisonitis with greater resilience.

7. Supports Authenticity and Personal Growth: Comparisonitis often pushes individuals towards conformity, as they strive to match the achievements or qualities of others. Self-compassion promotes authenticity by recognizing honour and ggoingone's unique path, talents, and aspirations. It allows individuals to focus on their personal growth and development, free from the pressure to constantly measure up to external standards.

8. Enhances Well-Being and Mental Health: Engaging in constant comparison can have detrimental effects on mental health and overall well-being. Self-compassion acts as a buffer against these negative impacts by fostering self-care, self-acceptance, and emotional well-being. It helps individuals cultivate a positive relationship with themselves, leading to increased happiness, satisfaction, and a greater sense of inner peace.

In combating comparisonitis, self-compassion serves as a transformative practice. By embracing self-compassion, individuals can counteract the negative effects of comparison, nurture their emotional well-being, and cultivate a healthier relationships with others

CHAPTER FOUR

Practical Steps in Overcoming Comparisonitis

Overcoming comparisonitis, the habit of constantly comparing oneself to others requires a proactive approach and a commitment to self-growth. By following practical steps, individuals can break free from the negative cycle of comparison and cultivate a healthier perspective. Here are the practical steps in overcoming comparisonitis:

1. Cultivate Self-Awareness: Begin by developing self-awareness and recognizing when comparisonitis arises within you. Pay attention to the triggers, thoughts, and emotions associated with comparison. Awareness allows you to catch yourself in the act of comparing and consciously choose to shift your mindset.

2. Challenge Unrealistic Standards: Question the unrealistic standards or ideals that you may be holding yourself to. Recognize that social media, societal pressures, and external influences often present an idealized and curated version of reality. Reframe your perspective by focusing on your unique qualities, strengths, and values instead of striving for an unattainable benchmark.

3. Practice Gratitude: Shift your focus from what you lack to what you appreciate in your own life. Cultivate a gratitude practice by regularly acknowledging and expressing gratitude for the blessings, achievements, and experiences you have. Gratitude helps foster contentment and reduces the need for comparison.

4. Set Personal Goals: Instead of comparing yourself to others, focus on setting personal goals and working towards them. Identify areas of growth and development that are meaningful to you. By directing your energy towards personal progress, you shift the focus from external comparisons to internal growth and fulfilment.

5. Celebrate Your Wins: Celebrate your achievements, no matter how small they may seem. Acknowledge your progress, milestones, and efforts along the way. Celebrating your wins reinforces a positive self-image and encourages self-validation, reducing the need for external validation through comparison.

6. Practice Self-Compassion: Be kind and understanding towards yourself. Treat yourself with the same compassion and empathy you would extend to a friend. Replace self-criticism with self-compassion, recognizing that everyone has their journey and that it's okay to make mistakes or face setbacks.

7. Limit Social Media Exposure: Recognize the impact that social media can have on comparisonitis. Take breaks from social media or limit your exposure if you find that it triggers negative comparisons. Be mindful of how you consume social media content and curate your feed to include positive and inspiring accounts.

8. Focus on Personal Growth: Prioritize your growth and development. Engage in activities, hobbies, or learning experiences that align with your interests and goals. Invest in self-improvement and focus on becoming the best version of yourself, rather than comparing yourself to others.

9. Cultivate a Supportive Network: Surround yourself with a supportive network of friends, mentors, or like-minded individuals who encourage personal growth and authenticity. Engage in meaningful conversations, seek advice and share experiences. A supportive network can provide perspective, guidance, and encouragement.

10. Practice Mindfulness: Cultivate mindfulness practices to stay present and non-judgmental. Be aware of your thoughts and emotions related to comparisonitis without attaching judgment or value to them. Mindfulness helps you detach from negative thought patterns and shift your focus back to the present moment.

11. Celebrate Others' Success: Instead of feeling threatened or envious of others' achievements, practice celebrating their success. Adopt an abundance mindset and genuinely support and uplift others. Shifting from a competitive mindset to a collaborative mindset fosters a positive and supportive environment.

12. Focus on Authenticity: Embrace your uniqueness and prioritize authenticity. Define success on your terms, based on your values and aspirations, rather than external comparisons. Allow your authentic self to shine through in all aspects of your life.

Overcoming comparisonitis is a personal journey that requires self-reflection and self-compassion.

CONCLUSION

Recap of The Impact of Comparisonitis

Comparisonitis can have a significant impact on various aspects of an individual's life and well-being. Here is a recap of the key impacts of comparisonitis:

1. Mental Health: Comparisonitis can negatively affect mental health by fueling feelings of inadequacy, low self-esteem, and self-doubt. Constantly comparing oneself to others can lead to increased levels of stress, anxiety, and depression.

2. Self-Esteem: Comparisonitis erodes self-esteem as individuals often perceive themselves as falling short in comparison to others. This can result in a diminished sense of self-worth and confidence.

3. Relationship Strain: Comparisonitis can strain relationships, both personal and professional. Constantly comparing oneself to others can create jealousy, resentment, and competition, leading to strained interactions and conflicts with others.

4. Unhappiness and Dissatisfaction: Engaging in comparisonitis often leads to a sense of unhappiness and dissatisfaction with one's own life. The focus on what others have or have achieved can overshadow personal accomplishments and the ability to find contentment in the present moment.

5. Procrastination and Paralysis: Comparisonitis can lead to a sense of overwhelm and a fear of failure. Individuals may become paralyzed by their self-doubt and the fear that they will never measure up to others, leading to procrastination and a lack of progress towards their goals.

6. Stifled Personal Growth: Comparisonitis hinders personal growth and development. Instead of focusing on their journey and progress, individuals may become consumed by comparing themselves to others. This can prevent them from taking risks, exploring new opportunities, and reaching their full potential.

7. Negative Self-Talk: Engaging in comparisonitis often involves negative self-talk and self-criticism. Individuals may develop a harsh internal dialogue, constantly berating themselves for not measuring up to perceived standards. This negative self-talk further reinforces feelings of inadequacy and self-doubt.

8. Impact on Well-being: Comparisonitis can take a toll on overall well-being. It can lead to increased stress levels, a diminished sense of happiness and fulfilment, and a general sense of dissatisfaction with one's life.

9. Inauthenticity: Comparisonitis can push individuals to adopt inauthentic behaviours and lifestyles in an attempt to match the achievements or qualities of others. This can lead to a loss of self-identity and a disconnection from one's true values and passions.

10. Lack of Enjoyment: Constantly comparing oneself to others can prevent individuals from fully enjoying and appreciating their own experiences and accomplishments. The focus on external comparisons can overshadow the joy and satisfaction that can be found in personal achievements and growth.

Recognizing and addressing the impact of comparisonitis is crucial for personal well-being and growth. By cultivating self-compassion, developing a growth mindset, and focusing on personal progress rather than external comparisons, individuals can overcome the negative effects of comparisonitis and create a more fulfilling and authentic life.

Encouragement to Prioritize Self-Compassion and a Growth Mindset

In the journey of self-improvement and personal development, it is essential to prioritize self-compassion and cultivate a growth mindset. These two powerful tools can greatly enhance your well-being, resilience, and ability to overcome challenges. Here is an encouragement to prioritize self-compassion and a growth mindset:

1. Embrace Self-Compassion: Be kind and gentle with yourself. Treat yourself with the same care and understanding you would offer to a close friend. Self-compassion means acknowledging your imperfections, mistakes, and setbacks without judgment or self-criticism. It involves extending love, empathy, and acceptance to yourself, especially during difficult times. Remember that self-compassion is not self-indulgence but a necessary practice for nurturing your emotional well-being.

2. Practice Self-Care: Prioritize self-care as an act of self-compassion. Take care of your physical, emotional, and mental well-being by engaging in activities that rejuvenate and energize you. This could include exercise, proper nutrition, quality sleep, engaging in hobbies, spending time in nature, or engaging in mindfulness practices. By nurturing yourself, you are better equipped to face challenges and maintain a positive mindset.

3. Cultivate a Growth Mindset: Embrace the belief that your abilities, skills, and intelligence are not fixed traits but can be developed through effort, perseverance, and learning. A growth mindset fosters resilience, a love for learning, and a willingness to embrace challenges as opportunities for growth. See failures and setbacks as valuable lessons and stepping stones towards success. Embrace a "yet" mindset, understanding that you may not have achieved something "yet," but with dedication and growth, you can progress.

4. Embrace Learning Opportunities: Seek out opportunities to learn and grow. Approach new experiences, skills, and knowledge with curiosity and a willingness to expand your horizons. Embrace challenges as opportunities to develop new strengths and overcome limitations. By continuously learning and expanding your abilities, you empower yourself to navigate life's uncertainties with confidence and adaptability.

5. Celebrate Progress, Not Perfection: Shift your focus from perfection to progress. Celebrate even the smallest victories and milestones along your journey. Recognize that growth and personal development are incremental processes, and each step forward is significant. Acknowledge your efforts, resilience, and the lessons learned along the way. By celebrating progress, you cultivate a positive mindset and reinforce the belief in your ability to overcome challenges.

6. Surround Yourself with Supportive People: Seek the company of supportive individuals who uplift and encourage you. Surround yourself with people who believe in your potential and provide constructive feedback. Engage in meaningful conversations that inspire growth, and collaborate with like-minded individuals who share similar goals and aspirations. A supportive network can offer valuable insights, motivation, and accountability.

7. Cultivate Mindfulness: Practice mindfulness to stay present and aware of your thoughts, emotions, and self-talk. Notice any self-limiting beliefs or negative patterns of comparison, and consciously choose to redirect your focus towards self-compassion and growth. By cultivating mindfulness, you can develop a greater sense of self-awareness, and consciously respond to challenges with kindness, resilience, and a growth-oriented mindset.

8. Set Meaningful Goals: Set goals that align with your values, passions, and personal growth. Break them down into actionable steps and create a plan to achieve them. As you work towards your goals, stay flexible and open to adjusting your approach as needed. Embrace the journey itself and avoir about the progress you make along the way.

Remember, prioritizing self-compassion and a growth mindset is a lifelong practice. Be patient with yourself, as it takes time and effort to develop these habits.

Printed in Great Britain
by Amazon

24831336R00046